BRITAIN IN PICTURES
THE BRITISH PEOPLE IN PICTURES

ENGLISH BALLET

GENERAL EDITOR
W. J. TURNER

ENGLISH BALLET

W. J. TURNER

WITH
8 PLATES IN COLOUR
4 PHOTOGRAPHS
AND
18 ILLUSTRATIONS IN
BLACK & WHITE

WILLIAM COLLINS OF LONDON
MCMXXXXIV

PRODUCED BY
ADPRINT LIMITED LONDON

PRINTED IN GREAT BRITAIN BY
CLARKE & SHERWELL LTD NORTHAMPTON
ON MELLOTEX BOOK PAPER MADE BY
TULLIS RUSSELL & CO LTD MARKINCH SCOTLAND

LIST OF ILLUSTRATIONS

PLATES IN COLOUR

PETROUCHKA
La Danseuse Triste by Alexandre Benois
Diaghileff—Stravinsky—Fokine. Paris 1911

ORIENTALES
Set designed for Anna Pavlova by Léon Bakst
Later used for Schéhérazade, Paris, 1910

HIGH YELLOW
Camargo Society—Spike Hughes—Buddy Bradley and Ashton. London, 1932
Design for the backcloth by Vanessa Bell

LE COQ D'OR
Diaghileff—Rimsky-Korsakov—Fokine. Paris, 1914
Design for a backcloth by Nathalie Gontcharova

THE WEDDING BOUQUET
Sadler's Wells. Ballet and music by Lord Berners. London, 1937

THE PROSPECT BEFORE US
Sadler's Wells—Boyce (arranged by Lambert)—Ninette de Valois. London, 1940
The stage of King's Theatre, 1789 : design for Scene I by Roger Furse

HAMLET
Sadler's Wells—Tchaikovsky—Helpmann. London, 1942
Design for the set by Leslie Hurry

THE QUEST
Sadler's Wells—Walton—Ashton. London, 1943
Design for the backcloth, Scene 3, by John Piper

PHOTOGRAPHS

LE LAC DES CYGNES, ACT IV
Margot Fonteyn, Robert Helpmann and Corps de Ballet
Décor by Leslie Hurry for the Sadler's Wells Company, 1943

THE WANDERER
Choreography by Frederick Ashton, décor by Graham Sutherland, music by Schubert
Sadler's Wells production, 1941

LES SYLPHIDES, THE OPENING PHRASE IN NOCTURNE
Décor by Ronald Wilson for the Ballet Rambert, 1944

MEPHISTO VALSE
Choreography by Frederick Ashton, décor by Sophie Fedorovitch, music by Liszt

BLACK AND WHITE ILLUSTRATIONS

PAGE

THE SLEEPING PRINCESS　5
Detail from the Tableau of Characters
by Nadia Benois
By courtesy of Arnold L. Haskell, Esq.

STUDY OF BALLET DANCERS OFF STAGE　7
Pen drawing by Christopher Wood
By courtesy of the Author

LARIONOV, PROKOFIEV AND DIAGHILEFF
AT A REHEARSAL　8
Pen and ink drawing by Larionov, Paris, 1921
By courtesy of Arnold L. Haskell, Esq.

BALLET DANCERS　11
Oil painting on panel by Christopher Wood
By courtesy of the Redfern Gallery

MADEMOISELLE CAMARGO　15
Engraving after the painting by N. Lancret
By courtesy of Madame Rambert

MARIE TAGLIONI　17
Engraving after A. E. Chalon
By courtesy of Madame Rambert

FANNY ELSSLER　19
Coloured engraving by M. Ganci after
J. Deffett Francis. Published 1838
By courtesy of Madame Rambert

COPPELIA ACT I　27
Costume design for Czardas Dancer by
William Chappell
By courtesy of the Sadler's Wells Company

LE LAC DES CYGNES　29
Costume design for the Mazurka by Leslie
Hurry
By courtesy of the Sadler's Wells Company

PAGE

MASSINE IN *TRICORNE*　31
Brush drawing by Theyre Lee-Elliott
By courtesy of the Artist

TAMARA KARSAVINA IN *THE TRUTH
ABOUT THE RUSSIAN DANCERS*　35
A play with ballet by J. M. Barrie, 1920
Design by Paul Nash
By courtesy of John Carr Doughty, Esq.

LES SYLPHIDES　37
Gouache by Theyre Lee-Elliott
By courtesy of the Artist

THE LADY AT THE WINDOW : *FAÇADE*　39
Design by John Armstrong
By courtesy of the Sadler's Wells Company

HAROLD TURNER IN *LES PATINEURS*　42
Gouache by Theyre Lee-Elliott
By courtesy of the Artist

MARGOT FONTEYN IN *NOCTURNE*　43
Gouache by Theyre Lee-Elliott
By courtesy of Miss Fonteyne and the Artist

SPECTRE DE LA ROSE　45
Design for the young girl's white ball
dress by Rex Whistler
By courtesy of the Sadler's Wells Company

COPPELIA　46
Design for the set, Act III, by William
Chappell
By courtesy of the Sadlers Wells Company

LE FESTIN DE L'ARAIGNEE　48
Costume design for the Praying Mantis
by Michael Ayrton
By courtesy of the Artist

STUDY OF BALLET DANCERS OFF STAGE
Pen drawing by Christopher Wood

INTRODUCTION

AS everybody knows we have as yet no English Opera as distinct from Opera in English, which we have had for very many years. There are people still living to-day who can remember the Moody-Manners Opera Company which, like the Carl Rosa Company, toured the provinces—with regular visits to the capital—and kept an interest in Opera alive in a wide public, a public quite distinct from the fashionable London audience which visited Covent Garden to hear famous foreign singers and conductors (and sometimes foreign orchestras) performing once a year there in a limited repertory of Italian, German, and French Opera. But it was also Italian, German, and French Opera which the Carl Rosa and the Moody-Manners Companies took to the provinces, for there was virtually no English Opera to take, and there had been none since the seventeenth century, when the last hope of our native Opera died in Henry Purcell. Throughout the eighteenth and nineteenth centuries, the nearest thing to Opera in this country was Light Opera, in imitation of Italian and French Comic Opera, and a sort of Ballad Opera in the tradition of Gay's *Beggar's Opera*. Our most famous example of light opera is the unique series created by the happy collaboration of that great wit W. S. Gilbert with the gifted composer Arthur Sullivan. The reasons for this relative sterility, as also for the general musical decline in this country since the seventeenth century, were largely sociological and political and need not be discussed here.

7

LARIONOV, PROKOFIEV AND DIAGHILEFF AT A REHEARSAL
Pen and ink drawing by Larionov, Paris 1921

Unlike opera, ballet had never been greatly in vogue here although dancing is as native to the English people as music, and in Elizabethan times was also wide-spread throughout the country. The Puritan influence stopped the development of festival dancing into an art, and in the eighteenth and nineteenth centuries ballet was only introduced into England from France and Italy as an entertainment, like opera, for the Court and the aristocracy. Naturally it was entirely foreign ballet with foreign dancers. If there had been a native art of ballet, these visits of ballet from abroad

PETROUCHKA
Diaghileff — Stravinsky — Fokine.   Paris 1911
La Danseuse Triste by Alexandre Benois

ORIENTALES
Set designed for Anna Pavlova by Léon Bakst

would have been greatly stimulating to our own dancers but we had none, and the public at large saw little or nothing of these foreign visitors, who came and went and left no trace behind them. In Russia, on the contrary, the Italian ballet brought to St. Petersburg and Moscow proved ultimately to be the source of a great national art of ballet in Russia, and it was, curiously enough, this birth of a National Russian ballet that became in due time the inspiration and direct cause of a similar birth of a national ballet in England.

Mr. Arnold Haskell has rightly said "The story of English ballet begins with Pavlova and Diaghileff"—in other words it begins with the Russians. Before this it was at the old variety halls like the Empire, the Palace Theatre and the Coliseum that the general public in the beginning of the twentieth century first became acquainted with great Continental dancers such as Adeline Genée and Lydia Kyasht. But these were individual star-dancers displaying their individual technique; their performances did not in the least constitute an art of ballet, although examples of nineteenth century French and Italian ballet were to be seen sporadically at the Old Alhambra in Leicester Square, as well as at Covent Garden annually during the opera season. Then in 1910 came the visit of Anna Pavlova from Russia. She was a revelation of what virtuoso dancing could be, and at the Palace Theatre in London, and in the provincial cities, she drew an immense new public. But her company of dancers were subordinate to her, and it was her solo-dancing as, for example, her unforgettable *Swan*, which was the real sensation. Her visits, however, achieved two important results: firstly she awakened a new interest in ballet-dancing, and stimulated much budding English talent. Throughout the country numbers of ambitious girls started to study ballet-dancing seriously who had never thought of it before, and Pavlova gave a fresh impetus to the schools of dancing here which for a long time had provided child dancers for pantomimes, and dancers for musical plays, and other spectacles. Secondly, when the Polish and Russian dancers in her company quarrelled, she introduced young English dancers, finding them excellent material. Recruits to our schools of dancing then began to come from sections of the public which, in the nineteenth century, would never have consented to let their children take up dancing as a serious profession. Pavlova, as a serious artist, helped to give prestige to ballet-dancing, for, as Mr. Haskell has written, "The tone she maintained in her company made it as respectable for a Colonel's daughter as any finishing school."

To Pavlova as a Russian dancer trained in the Great Imperial School at St. Petersburg (still maintained at Leningrad) there was nothing new in this. Those who have read Madame Karsavina's delightful Memoirs will remember her fascinating account of the strict training and discipline—as rigorous as that of a Guards regiment—which prevailed at that great Russian ballet school, which has turned out the finest dancers in the world for more than half a century. So far, however, the visits of Pavlova had merely stimulated the English public's interest in the virtuoso side of ballet dancing, for the technique of Pavlova was a revelation of what virtuoso dancing might be. No idea of what the *art* of ballet might be, however, had yet dawned upon even the most enlightened of the British public. This was to come very quickly after the visits of Pavlova, beginning in 1910, with the first appearance in London of Diaghileff's Russian Ballet in 1911.

Then followed a memorable season in 1913 at Drury Lane. Russian ballet and opera were sponsored by Sir Joseph Beecham, the millionaire father of Sir Thomas Beecham. It was then that the new art of Russian ballet, as developed by the genius of Diaghileff, burst upon an astonished world—first of all in Paris, then in London, to spread later to America and the Dominions, as far as Australia. This has been indisputably the greatest artistic sensation of our time, and many people can still remember vividly the astonishment of the audiences which first saw such ballets as *The Firebird, Petrouchka,* and *Le Sacre de Printemps*. These ballets were a revelation to all for whom, up to then, ballet had meant at its best, stereotyped performances of *Coppélia, Giselle* and other famous ballets of the nineteenth century; or, at its ordinary level, tasteless or commonplace spectacles at the music halls.

Diaghileff's original work was firmly rooted in the great classical tradition, just as all the best new work in every art is; but nevertheless, he was a pioneer, for he combined a remarkable degree of taste in all the three separate arts of music, dancing and painting. He began as a rich connoisseur of painting in Russia, and became a leader in the world of art there; he had a rare individual judgment which enabled him to pick out comparatively unknown men and he dared to take the risk of commissioning work from them. Unlike so many connoisseurs and amateurs, he had both real knowledge and an almost infallible instinct, and was accepted by all artists—whether painters, musicians, or dancers—as one of them. Consequently, he was able to get men of original talent, such as Stravinsky, Manuel de Falla, Satie, Prokofiev among musicians; Bakst, Derain, Picasso, Braque, Benois, among painters; Nijinska, Fokine, Nijinsky, Massine and Cecchetti among choreographers to combine to produce ballets which were works of art conceived as a whole in a way that was unique. Like the work of most

BALLET DANCERS
Oil painting on panel by Christopher Wood

pioneers, Diaghileff's efforts did not pay. Everywhere they made an artistic sensation, but they were much too novel for the general public, and always had to be financed by educated and wealthy patrons. Gradually, however, the influence of these remarkable works spread, and nowhere more fruitfully than in England.

In 1922, the Cecchetti Society was formed to preserve this great dancer's teaching in England. In 1923 an English dancer Alice Marks made a success as Markova, and she and Ninette de Valois joined the Diaghileff Ballet. In 1926 Frederick Ashton, an English dancer, produced his first ballet *The Tragedy of Fashion* and Ninette de Valois opened an Academy of Choreographic Art. In 1929 Diaghileff died and the following year the Camargo Society (named after the great Italian dancer, 1710-1770) was

11

founded; with this Society Marie Rambert's company of dancers, trained at her London school, were associated. Marie Rambert started her own Ballet club at the little Mercury Theatre at Notting Hill Gate in London and her company still creates interesting work, developing young dancers and choreographic talent and touring the provinces. The Camargo Society had the support of the Russian dancer Lydia Lopokova who had made her London reputation under Diaghileff in *La Boutique Fantasque* and had married the present Lord Keynes. She and her husband have been among the strongest and most constant supporters of English ballet. The Camargo Society produced some of the first and most important English Ballets, namely, *Job*, *Façade*, and *Rio Grande*, thus bringing the English composers Vaughan Williams, William Walton, and Constant Lambert into the sphere of national ballet. Actually our national ballet may be said to have been founded in 1931 on the formation of a permanent company by that remarkable woman, Lilian Bayliss, at the Sadler's Wells Theatre under Ninette de Valois. The tremendous and continual success of this company is now well known.

The reputation of the Sadler's Wells Ballet reached the Continent and an invitation came to visit Holland, as a result of which a tour was arranged for 1940. For the following description of what happened I am indebted to Miss Amabel Farjeon who was a member of the *corps de ballet* at the time.

"The Sadler's Wells Ballet tour of Holland, Belgium and the Western Front was brought to an abrupt close after its fourth performance. The first night in the Hague we had been showered with flowers; the second night in Hengelo, a few miles from the German frontier, we had been spat and jeered at in the street, and two days later on the morning of May 10th, just returned from Arnhem, we were awakened after an hour's rest by the roar of planes and gun-fire over the Hague.

"While those responsible busied themselves with schemes for the escape, we dancers engrossed ourselves as best we could during the alternate periods of tiresome inaction and frantic stir; the latter created by such events as being shot at in a café, it was rumoured by a fifth columnist; or machine-gunned on the roof, while watching Rotterdam burn and parachutists drop through the sunny morning air (this bird's-eye view had made it seem as remote from reality as a military tattoo). During the delay, boredom drove the dancers to devise their own amusements, the originality of which revealed how far the intensive ballet training had taken effect, virtually cutting them off from normal life. Suddenly faced with the grim actuality of war, there was an extraordinary combination of cowardice, hysteria and humour.

LE LAC DES CYGNES, ACT IV

Margot Fonteyn, Robert Helpmann and Corps de Ballet

Décor by Leslie Hurry for the Sadler's Wells Company, 1943

Photograph by Tunbridge-Sedgwick

THE WANDERER
Choreography by Frederick Ashton, décor by Graham Sutherland, music by Schubert
Sadler's Wells production, 1941
Photograph by Gordon Anthony

"By the time the German army had made its way well into Holland, we were still trapped in the Hague. The company performed physical jerks to the B.B.C. programme of 'Up in the Morning Early' in the pompous hotel lounge, before an astonished audience of depressed Dutch business men. But as the hours wore on there were nervous climaxes, again relieved by Frederick Ashton or Robert Helpmann's irresistible humour, when white and worried faces would lift with laughter, and the mind could picture Dutch and Germans, anxious relations in England, and the company itself quite objectively as comedy characters in a fantastic world farce.

"That night the time came to leave, and we travelled in a bus for nine hours, with not the least idea of where we were going, crammed in with the luggage so tightly that it was only just possible to cross or uncross our legs, to twist a little for conversation. As a result of this unhappy situation there was despondency and alarm: Robert Helpmann was filled with serious consternation on seeing the new moon through glass; later, when someone laughed, Claude Newman mentioned that 'it was not the time for hilarity.' The bus got lost, chased by an armed patrol, while distant fires of the advancing enemy lit the night skyline, and guns shook the air, blasting above the rattle of the engine.

"In the end we stopped at a pension at Velsen, where the stables were taken over by the military, the house itself being filled with other refugees. During the day's waiting for a chance to get through to the harbour of Ijmuiden, we wandered about lovely grounds, revived and gay once more —perhaps because we were accustomed to make quick recoveries from physical exhaustion, for our fellow refugees appeared listless. The girls rejoiced that there were no tights to wash or darn, no sore toes to doctor; while the boys found a football and kicked it around on the grass. Some of the Dutch soldiers joined in, and there developed a serious game between the army and the ballet.

Being unable to speak each other's language seemed no handicap, for there were the commonly understood rules of football which sufficed. The two sides were well matched, and it was most amusing to see the glib and cynical ballet boys revert to the public school tradition of their country, suddenly imbued with such a 'team spirit' as rises in the Englishman playing for his honour against a foreigner.

"Quick and light the ballet tore about the grass, while the older Dutchmen, in their army boots, plunged and kicked heavily. A soldier on guard grew so worried and excited because his side was losing, that he joined in, racing up and down fully equipped till he nearly ran Alan Carter through with the bayonet, which had remained slung over his shoulder.

"It was late that night, during a lull in the gun fire and planes, when we were shown out and, in a hush of fear, got in the bus once more. I was told that it took three hours to do the three miles to Ijmuiden; but in that journey all sense of time was lost, for every now and again there would be shots outside, the company would pile into heaps in the gangway, the bus would pull up with a jolt and the guard would lift his rifle and rest the barrel on the window ledge. Such moments of terrified expectation, waiting for the bang when the guard fired and the splintering glass seemed endless.

"Morning came, and we were half way to England in the hold of a cargo ship. The ballet, combing straws out of its hair, shaking the creases from its clothes, wandered on deck and, in the grey green light, girls dabbed lipstick and powder over their worn and dirty faces. This gave one a sense of coming back to normal, despite its sordid incongruity with the situation. Constant Lambert appeared out of the luggage piles, looking most dramatic with a large bandage round his head; but this was not the result of the heroism one immediately suspected—a burning cigar ash had fallen into his eye while he lay smoking.

"Having had no money with which to buy food in the later stages of our adventure, we had not eaten properly for forty-eight hours. Hungry and dirty we mooched around the decks, watching the battleship that plunged ahead through the pale sea. But a large and comfortable looking Dutch family sat up on the hatches eating its breakfast, and some instinct or rumour seemed to draw the whole company to this place, till we were congregated about the party at an only-just-decent distance, steadily watching each mouthful taken. Whether it was our hungry stare that worried their consciences I don't know, but patience was rewarded for, when they had at length finished, each of us was handed a slice of dry bread and garlic sausage. Somewhat abashed we separated and, standing against the rail chewing, saw land a faint blur between the sea and sky.

"Our journey was coming to a close. Looking back it was possible to realise the pattern of circumstances, and how Ninette de Valois always stood out, carrying the weight of responsibility. Looking forward, towards England, it was only possible to visualise a good meal and a warm bed."

Since 1940 the Company has toured the provinces regularly and given frequent seasons every year at the New Theatre, London. It has discovered new British talent in composers, choreographers, artists and dancers, and its success has, I hope, come to stay. In no other country in the world has the Diaghileff revival of the art of ballet had a comparable offspring and it is no exaggeration to say that to-day England and Russia lead the world in the creative renaissance of this delightful art.

MADEMOISELLE CAMARGO
Engraving after the painting by N. Lancret

ORIGINS

BEFORE giving in any detail an account of the art of Ballet in England since the foundation of a National School of Ballet at Sadler's Wells a brief account of the art itself, its origins and its historic development is called for. The origin of Ballet as a separate art almost synchronises with that of Opera. Both are products of the Renaissance in Europe, which came after a long period of incubation following the decline and fall of the Roman Empire when the great migrations of the barbarians swept across Europe destroying the old classic civilisations. Christianity slowly introduced light into the dark chaos of the times and, as Christianity spread westwards, the Feudal System also emerged bringing with it a new settled order of society. It was not until this process of social re-organisation had gone such a long way that national states (England, France and Spain, for example) had begun to emerge and—in the Italian peninsula as well as east of the Rhine—many powerful cities and principalities were enjoying security and material prosperity, that men in these settled communities began to have the leisure and peace of mind to ask themselves once again how they might live more richly and fully. Curiosity as to how life had been lived in the past was awakened, the desire for knowledge, which had been sustained and nourished only in isolated monasteries and courts throughout the Middle Ages, now increased wherever trade, commerce and a strong government flourished.

By the middle of the fifteenth century that re-discovery by scholars and artists of the great civilisations of Greece and Rome was in full flood. Nowhere was it more evident than in Italy where at the Courts of the most powerful Princes and Dukes, in Papal Rome, and in Florence (that great centre of merchant Princes such as the Medici family) an intense artistic activity now flourished. Architecture, philosophy and literature were all being studied with minds awakened to new ideas by the ancient manu-scripts brought by Greek scholars escaping westwards after the capture of Constantinople by the Saracens in 1453 Aristotle, Plato and the great Greek dramatists were being translated and the marvellous cultural creation of the Greeks shone suddenly like a lighthouse to guide mankind by dispersing the fogs of superstition and ignorance which had enveloped the Middle Ages. The importance given by the Greeks in their literature to music inspired the Italians to try to restore its role in the Greek presentation of drama by means of *Le Nuove Musiche* (The New Music) or *Dramma per Musica* (Drama through Music). Music had become over-intellectualized and abstract. Ingenuity and complication had paralyzed expression and the New Music was to change all this, just as experiment was to break the barriers of scholasticism to open new gateways to scientific thinking. Greek mythological subjects provided the first fresh material and in 1597 the composer Peri wrote the first opera *Dafne* which was soon followed by others by Caccini, and Monteverde, whose *Orpheus* was produced at Mantua in 1607. Now we know that choreographic dances with a religious significance had been part of the ancient classical drama of Greece. In fact the dramatic works of the great trio of Greek dramatists—Aeschylus, Sophocles and Euripides, as well as those of the comic writers, were founded on earlier ritual miming and dancing at purely religious festivals. Such ritual dances go back to pre-historic times and are to be found everywhere among primitive races throughout the world. In them the art of ballet finds its earliest origins, and indeed music and ballet go back to the beginnings of human history, as I shall show in more detail later.

Miming accompanied by musical declamation made up the two chief ingredients of the earliest operas but as music developed as an art its

MARIE TAGLIONI
Engraving after A. E. Chalon

importance in opera became paramount, and as the miming and dancing also developed parallel with music they in turn demanded freedom from subordination to music and drama, and thus ballet was born as a separate art. Some historians declare that the first ballet was the *Ballet Comique de la Reine* given at Versailles in 1581 to celebrate the marriage of Margaret of Lorraine, sister of Henri III of France with the Duc de Joyeuse. In the reign of Henri IV (1589-1610) eighty grand ballets were given at the French

17

Court and under Louis XIV the famous dancing master Beauchamp, and the composer Lully, collaborated in numerous ballets, while the King himself founded a Royal Academy of Dancing in Paris in 1661.

The art of ballet took to itself most of the popular dance forms such as chaconnes, gigues, gavottes, minuets, bourrées, etc. The ladies of the court danced; but it is believed that no woman appeared as a dancer on a public stage in Europe until about 1681. Another feature of seventeenth and eighteenth century ballet was that even when the characters represented came from Greek and Roman mythology they were always dressed in the costumes of the day. Marie Sallé caused a sensation in London in 1734 by appearing as Pygmalion in a muslin dress without the conventional head-dress. To the great ballerina Camargo, who from 1726 to 1751 was the idol of the public, we owe the introduction of ballet slippers and shorter skirts which, however, were longer than the now classic skirt as they still fell below the knee. Toe-dancing was an even later development and did not come in until about 1830, when Taglioni and Elssler became its chief exponents; and bare-foot dancing was first introduced by the American, Isodora Duncan, about 1906. Tights were invented in the nineteenth century by a Paris costumier named Maillot so that what we now consider the classic ballet costume, as worn in famous ballets such as *Le Lac des Cygnes* or *Coppélia* is a comparatively recent invention; nor is it one that is ever likely to be superseded as it achieves the maximum of freedom with beauty of line. Here it may be mentioned as an interesting fact that owing to the difference in the physical conformation of the ankles of men and women toe-dancing is much more difficult for men, which is one of the reasons why the role of the male dancer became subordinate to that of the woman dancer in ballet throughout the nineteenth century.

In this short sketch of the origins of the art of ballet it only remains to say that in England the chief examples of ballet during the seventeenth century were incorporated into the form of Masques—which reached perhaps a greater development in this country than anywhere else, especially in the reign of James I, when authors such as Ben Jonson, Fletcher, Beaumont, Chapman, Dekker, Shirley and Milton (whose *Comus* was performed in 1634 at Ludlow Castle), architects, such as Inigo Jones, and musicians such as Ferrabosco, Campion, Lawes and Locke combined to produce the most sumptuous and elaborate works in which drama, music, dancing and architectural machinery were more or less happily combined. But this marked the end of national ballet as it more or less did of national opera in England until the beginning of the twentieth century. Ballet as seen in England during the eighteenth and nineteenth centuries was almost

FANNY ELSSLER
Coloured engraving by M. Ganci after J. Deffett Francis. Published 1838

entirely of foreign origin and was executed by foreign artists visiting this country.

It is not only the sciences but also the arts that become more and more specialised in the course of time. The first ballet undoubtedly must have taken place as a ritual or festival dance to a primitive form of music chiefly rhythmical with little melodic shape and without harmony. So strangely do old things become new again that Stravinsky's very sophisticated Russian ballet *Le Sacre de Printemps* (*Spring Rite*), first produced in 1913 was an attempt to recapture something of the mood and primitive character of one of these dance-festivals, which were tribal celebrations of a sacred nature occurring before the dawn of history or art. Such religious festivals --which are always originally linked with natural phenomena, such as the return of spring, midsummer, the approach of winter; or with the principal events in the life of primitive man, such as hunting, sowing, or harvesting—still occur in parts of the East, in India, in Australia and Polynesia, in Central Africa and also in Central and South America. We may call them primitive, using the word in its literal sense of early; but we must be careful to rid our minds of any suggestion of the undeveloped or the inferior in using this word here; for, on the contrary, from an aesthetic and religious point of view this kind of ritual dancing probably often achieved the highest point of development dancing has so far reached in the expression of human emotions. I myself once witnessed a performance of dancers, with their musicians, from a region of Africa still largely unaffected by European or American influence, which for dramatic intensity and a quality of imaginative wonder far surpassed any contemporary art-ballet. There are parts of India and the East, too, where native performances of a similar grandeur and authenticity can still be seen, and it is indeed the contemplation of such things that made a man like Gandhi so anxious to preserve and develop the native culture of India and to prevent its extinction by an inferior imitation of an alien European and American culture; a conservatism more particularly necessary when it is conceivable that this western culture is itself in a temporarily decadent stage. But decadence and renewal are perhaps no farther apart in art than in nature and so it was therefore only natural that the effect on sensitive artists in Europe and America of Stravinsky's *Spring Rite* was tremendous, coming as it did from the depths of man's history; indeed, it would be no exaggeration to say it was an artistic bombshell shattering the traditional conceptions of the ballet form.

Fear and wonder were probably the dominating emotions of men in primitive societies. With urban civilisation it seems as if they have diminished in intensity. I say *seems* but many, no doubt, would be more emphatic and say this was certainly so. Yes, for the majority, perhaps, but one must not forget that the imaginative capacity of wonder is just what makes poets and artists creative, and it would be certainly rash to suppose that men like Wordsworth, Shakespeare, Rembrandt and Michelangelo were inferior in this capacity for imaginative wonder even to the men who hundreds of thousands of years ago drew the animals in the Altamira caves, or welcomed the return of Spring with a Corn Dance. Pleasure in the exercise of the body and of the mind in doing and making remains still, as it has always been, the chief good of life, and naturally all early dance festivals not connected with the act of wonder (or what in modern religions is called 'worship') are festivals of eating, drinking and sexual intercourse; there being always in a healthy normal activity an easy transition from the

LES SYLPHIDES, THE OPENING PHRASE IN NOCTURNE
Décor by Ronald Wilson for the Ballet Rambert, 1944
Photograph by Peggy Delius

MEPHISTO VALSE
Choreography by Frederick Ashton, décor by Sophie Fedorovitch, music by Liszt
Photograph by Tunbridge-Sedgwick

imagination of the act to the act itself. Perhaps I could not do better than quote here from a poem of mine entitled *The Ritual Dance*, which was an attempt to describe such a festival.

THE RITUAL DANCE

In the black glitter of night the grey vapour forest
Lies a dark ghost in the water, motionless, dark,
Like a corpse by the bank fallen, and hopelessly rotting
Where the thin silver soul of the stars silently dances.

The flowers are closed, the birds are carved on the trees,
When out of the forest glide hundreds of spear-holding shadows,
In smooth dark ivory bodies their eyeballs gleaming,
Forming a gesturing circle beneath the Moon.

The bright-eyed Shadows, the tribe in ritual gathered,
Are dancing and howling, the embryo soul of a nation:
In loud drum-beating monotonous the tightly stretched skins
Of oxen that stared at the stars are singing wild pæans:

Wild pæans for food that magically grew in the clearings
When he that was slain was buried and is resurrected,
And a green mist arose from the mud and shone in the Moon,
A great delirium of faces, a new generation.

The thin wafer Moon it is there, it is there in the sky,
The hand-linked circle raise faces of mad exultation—
Dance, O you Hunters, leap madly upon the flung shields,
Shoot arrows into the sky, thin moon-seeking needles:

Now you shall have a harvest, a belly-full rapture,
There shall be many fat women, full grown, and smoother than honey,
Their lips full of food and their eyes full of hunger for men!

The heat of the earth arises, a faint love mist
Wan with over-desiring, and in the marshes
Blindly the mud stirs, clouding the dark shining water,
And troubling the still soft swarms of fallen stars.

There is bright sweat upon the bodies of cattle,
Great vials of life motionless in the moon-light,
Breathing faint mists over the warm, damp ground;
And the cry of a dancer rings through the shadowy forest.

21

The tiger is seeking his mate and his glassy eyes
Are purple and shot with starlight in the grass shining,
The fiery grass tortured out of the mud and writhing
Under the sun, now shivering and pale in the Moon.

The shadows are dancing, dancing, dancing, dancing:
The grey vapour arms of the forest lie dreaming around them;
The cold, shining moonlight falls from their bodies and faces,
But caught in their eyes lies prisoned and faintly gleaming:

And they return to their dwellings within the grey forest,
Into their dark huts, burying the moonlight with them,
Burying the trees and the stars and the flowing river,
And the glittering spears, and their dark, evocative gestures.

SLEEP

Hollow the world in the moonlit hour when the birds are shadows small,
Lost in the swarm of giant leaves and myriad branches tall;
When vast thick boughs hang across the sky like solid limbs of night,
Dug from still quarries of grey-black air by the pale transparent light,
And the purple and golden blooms of the sun, each crimson and spotted
                                        flower,
Are folded up or have faded away, as that still intangible power
Floats out of the sky, falls shimmering down, a silver-shadowed bloom,
On the spear-pointed forest a fragile crown, in the soul a soft white bloom;
Hollow the world when the shadow of man lies prone and still on its floor,
And the moonlight shut from his empty heart weeps softly against his
                                        door,
And his terror and joy but a little dream in the corner of his house,
And his voice dead in the darkness 'mid the twittering of a mouse.

From this attempt to render the atmosphere of primitive ritual-dancing
we may catch some notion of what those early ritual dances were like, and
realise how deeply they expressed the emotional life of the people, and
what great satisfaction they found in them.

When metaphysicians debate whether anything exists outside the
mind that imagines it, the artist is content to believe that reality is dual,
and is always an *object-subject* phenomenon, it being impossible for mere
'objects' or mere 'subjects' to exist by themselves. So to him the image
and the emotion (or the thought and the thinker) are one; but a living,

that is a changing one, and it is this living relationship that is given expression in art.

As far as our historic knowledge goes it is possible that we might claim the great Greek classical dramas—both tragedy and comedy—as a kind of ballet-opera in which traditional heroic events of the peoples' early history, or legend were celebrated for their edification, as well as in honour of the gods. Certainly miming and dancing were important elements in these dramas, as they were in the much later 'No' plays of Japan and in the Biblical dramatic representations throughout Europe in the Middle Ages; culminating in the Mystery and Morality plays which foreshadowed the more specialised forms of drama of the Renaissance. For it was not until the sixteenth and seventeenth centuries that a more absolute specialisation developed into the three distinct forms of Drama, Ballet and Opera, and even then they were often intermingled. Ballet has even remained as an incidental appanage of opera right up to our own time, in spite of the objections made occasionally by purists who think the mixture a menace to the proper integrity and development of one or other art. Wagner, for example, much against his will, introduced a ballet into *Tannhäuser*, and an example of an elaborate ballet included in a late nineteenth century work is to be found in Verdi's opera, *Aïda*. It is only comparatively recently, since the late eighteenth century, that ballet has been estimated for its own sake as a separate and individual art form, a position which it had once before, then lost, and has begun only in our own time fully to regain.

THE ELEMENTS OF BALLET

MODERN Ballet is a combination of dancing, music, plot and *décor*. By *décor* is meant the scenery or visual setting of the dancing, including the costumes. It is obvious that we are not all equally susceptible to each of these elements. This is the chief reason why there is such a diversity of opinion about the merit of any particular ballet. For some the dancing, for some the music, and for others the visual scene predominates in interest. Only a small minority are equally sensitive and receptive to all these elements; on the other hand all normal men and women have at least a rudimentary development of the visual and auditory senses and get some pleasure from each. This pleasure can be enormously increased by practice and attention. The more you know, the more you enjoy; the more you see the more you find there is to see; and the more perceptive your hearing the richer becomes the world of sound. To enjoy fully all which the art of ballet has to offer, you must become an enthusiast, but a discriminating enthusiast who is, at least to some degree, aware of the contribution each element makes to the effect of the whole.

I propose now to discuss in some detail the four elements that go to make a ballet, and then to illustrate them with an analysis of particular examples. I will take them in the following order: (1) dancing, (2) music, (3) *décor*, and (4) plot, although it may be contended that there is no historic, chronological order since these four elements have been inseparable from the beginning, and no one of them is later in origin than another. For example, in the earliest religious festival celebrations, even among the most primitive peoples, dancing was accompanied with music—if it were only a rhythmic beating of tom-toms. Nor did these primitive dancers on these occasions wear their ordinary dress, such as it was. No, they wore special costumes and elaborate head-dresses and painted themselves in a variety of colours, and often represented themselves as birds or animals with an astonishing degree of inventive pictorial fantasy. Their dancing would have been shorn of most of its glamour and effect if the dancers had worn their conventional everyday attire. Most early dancing is mimetic and dramatic; at the beginning there is very little dancing that is purely formal and gymnastic. By 'gymnastic' I mean purely formal physical movements displaying the beauty of the human body; its design as an inverted cone balanced marvellously on, as it were, a point, and yet able to move and bend and gesture in all directions with great rapidity and grace without collapse. Appreciation of the extraordinary beauty of the human figure and its mobility in its upright position (a sort of persistent infringement of the Law of Gravitation) first came to be fully appreciated in historic times by the ancient Greeks, and theirs is the first sculpture that reveals a direct attention to this formal phenomenon. Most of the earlier sculpture of the Egyptians, for example, shows no trace of it, betraying as it does an almost exclusively static quality, and a preoccupation with the emotional intensity of inward religious feeling. Thus, Egyptian sculpture frequently portrays seated figures; there is nothing for example, resembling the Greek disc-thrower, and certainly we may say that just as mobility characterises the Greek feeling for sculpture so Egyptian sculpture (at its most individual and significant period) is static, immobile and even oppressively weighty.

Italy, with its classic background and in its renaissance of the classical tradition, became not surprisingly, the natural home of the first development in Europe of dancing as an art in itself, an entertainment enjoyed for its own sake and not as a religious rite. Once one realises fully the geometric

24

HIGH YELLOW

Camargo Society — Spike Hughes — Buddy Bradley and Ashton.   London 1932

Design for the backcloth by Vanessa Bell

LE COQ D'OR

Diaghileff — Rimsky-Korsakov — Fokine.   Paris Opera 1914.   Revived as a Ballet by de Basil, London 1937

Design for a backcloth by Nathalie Gontcharova

similarity of the human body to an inverted cone, a cone standing on its pointed and narrowest end, one perceives immediately how natural and inevitable was the Italian invention of toe-dancing, late as it was. These pointed ballet-shoes which add inches to the dancer's height, which make this sustained poise both more graceful and more precarious are a logical development to render more striking the wonderful symmetry and power of control of the human body, and to emphasise the dancer's lightness and mobility.

Much of our immediate and deepest pleasure in ballet-dancing proceeds from this apparent defiance of the law of gravitation by the ballet-dancer on points. This may be called a technical interest, and toe-dancing is certainly a foundation-technique of ballet. This technique, however, is relatively modern, dating only from about 1830 and it is a technique for which women are more physically suited than men—owing, as I have said, to the slightly different formation of their ankles.

Now it is only necessary to watch with close attention the feet and legs of solo dancers in any of the classical nineteenth century ballets such as *Coppélia* to begin to appreciate the refinements of this technique. The variation in control and grace is astonishing; but it will need a more than casual eye to notice it. A casual observer will never discern what distinguishes a Pavlova from the most ordinary member of a *corps de ballet*. Once the eye has been trained to perceive the leg and foot technique then the observer's attention may gradually extend to include the trunk, the arms and the head. All the subtlest modes of expression are manifested through the upper limbs of the body, the arms and head; but they need a firm foundation, an absolute sureness of foot and leg before they can develop their utmost powers of expression; it is in the arms and head that the genius of the dancer finds its ultimate most delicate and intensest expression. A close attention to the movements and poses of the head, arms and hands of a dancer will reveal those great differences such as we may find (if we have a poetic instinct and literary training) in poetry, which always mark the major from the minor artist.

So far I have been speaking of the body, of physical movement only, but do not let us mistake the physical for the inferior. Everything, even the highest, most subtle and refined of spiritual ideas and feelings can and do need to find a physical expression. No musical instrument ever invented can equal or even approach the human body as an effective vehicle for thought and feeling, but psychological perversion masquerading as religious fervour has spoiled for many generations the pure and direct appreciation of the body's beauty. In Great Britain and other Protestant countries, a proper perception of pure beauty, and especially of the natural beauty of men and women, has been ruined by vulgarity and crank sexual fears and inhibitions. It is one of the secrets of the immense appeal nowadays of the ballet that it has nothing of this vulgar crudity, and thus has brought back to ordinary people (just as, in a different way, athletics have) the supremely satisfying and natural sense of physical beauty, and its dignity.

I shall not trouble the reader with detailed explanations of the technical names for the various ballet steps—the *pirouettes*, *fouettés*, *entrechats* etc. used in ballet manuals, or with a description of the written notation which has been invented to convey the choreography of the ballet from one master to another. These are quite unimportant and unnecessary for the layman, just as a knowledge of a musical notation is not required for a highly developed understanding and enjoyment of music. It is the eyes, and the mind behind the eyes, that are important. To be able to *see* distinctly more and more detail, that is the essential—the names given to the details seen do not matter. Just in the same way, it is the *ear* that matters in music. It is quite superfluous, quite beside the point, to know the names of chords or keys but very important to *hear* the differences between them. To *know* the words 'counterpoint' and 'fugue' is merely to add more words to one's vocabulary with the almost certain risk of misusing them; but it is vitally important to *hear* counterpoint and to distinguish the different threads in the contrapuntally woven harmony. It is a fact that the purely musical perception is, in general, so rudimentary among even educated music-lovers that the majority are only aware of the emotional colour of the music they enjoy; they rarely attain to a development of their purely musical intelligence sufficient to enable them genuinely to perceive for instance, the superiority of a fine piece of Puccini to one of his more vulgar cater-waulings. Similarly, for everyone who fully perceives the plastic subtlety and expressive beauty of the solo dances in for example, *Le Lac des Cygnes* there are likely to be more who will be moved by the dramatic miming of Mr. Robert Helpmann (or any other equally gifted mime) in his *Hamlet* ballet. But this is only to say that the dramatic (and above all the melo-dramatic) is easier to appreciate than the lyric and formal elements in all the arts.

But whoever develops a taste for ballet will find that the more they see the more they become aware of the inexhaustible delights of plastic forms. And not only the forms of the exquisitely proportioned, disciplined, and balanced physical bodies of the individual dancers; nor (as a second stage) the rhythmic beauty of their movements and the elaborated technique of the solo ballet dancer, but also (stage three) the inexhaustible richness of

26

COPPELIA ACT I
Costume design for Czardas Dancer by William Chappell

possible groupings of dancers in innumerable patterns either as foreground, background, or as an integrated rhythmic complement to the action of the solo dancers. This use of the *corps de ballet* by a talented choreographer may be compared with a musician's gift of instrumentation or orchestration. There is a striking example of it in Marius Petipa's choreography of Act II of *Le Lac des Cygnes*. Further developments of this orchestrated grouping occur in Massine's ballet *Choreartium* (using the music of Brahm's Fourth Symphony); in his *Les Présages* (with Tchaikovsky's Fifth Symphony), and in his choreography to Berlioz's *Symphonie Fantastique*.

Here is the place for a brief explanation of the word choreography which derives from two Greek words *choros*—dance and *graphein*—write. So choreography means the design of the dance, the plan of the ballet based on a plot, that is a story, an idea, or a situation. The fourth element, therefore, of plot, although it provides nothing more than the germ of a ballet, and is though primal yet of minor importance in the ultimate effect of the ballet as a whole, is nevertheless important enough to be reckoned as a separate, fourth element. But the talent of the choreographer is shown not so much in his choice or invention (which last is extremely rare) of a plot, as in his handling of it, in his contriving varied and expressive dances and groupings and rhythmic plastic combinations of his principals with the *corps de ballet*. His is, on the whole, the most important role in the art of ballet and nearly always he himself is, or has been, a dancer, and must understand thoroughly the technique of dancing. The really talented choreographer is sufficiently rare for me to be able to name here the chief choreographers of our time, namely, Petipa, Fokine, Cecchetti, Nijinsky, Nijinska, Massine, Balanchine, Ninette de Valois and Frederick Ashton, who is the only Englishman ever to have done a work for the Russians. Among younger people who have shown great promise and a certain definite achievement are Robert Helpmann, Anthony Tudor and Andrée Howard.

To the choreographer next in importance to the understanding of dancing comes a musical sense. It is the marriage of music and dancing in a unity which is something other and more than either of them alone that constitutes the essence of ballet, and the success of the visual element of *décor* depends entirely upon how far it aids and enhances the character of that achieved unity of idea and expression.

When I saw the new *décor* for *Le Lac des Cygnes* by the English artist Leslie Hurry I was struck by the remarkable way it enhanced the strange romantic atmosphere of the second act of Tchaikovsky's masterpiece. Hurry's design is dark and cavernous, lit from a ghost-like swan in its far-distant back-stage opening. When the Sadler's Wells Ballet commissioned Leslie Hurry to design the new *décor* for *Swan Lake* I thought it was a mistake. It seemed to me that the artist who designed the magnificent hot, lurid, nightmarish *Hamlet* for Robert Helpmann was not the person to do justice to the strange fairy-like though exotically romantic Tchaikovsky ballet, but I was wrong. Mr. Hurry proved to be more versatile

LE LAC DES CYGNES
The Mazurka. Costume designs by Leslie Hurry

and sensitive than I had expected and in fact his setting of *Swan Lake* is as successful as his *Hamlet*.

It was Diaghileff who opened up new possibilities in *décor*. He freed ballet from the conventional pretty-pretty and the equally conventional ugly, heavy and tasteless elaboration of the Victorian and Edwardian ages.

29

Such a masterpiece of simple and austere beauty as Picasso's setting of *The Three Cornered Hat*, for example, had never before been seen on any stage in the world. Many of Diaghileff's latest triumphs in ballet were mainly visual triumphs, triumphs of *décor*, for in a number of cases the choreography and the idea of the ballet were not on the same level, being often more freakish and startling than interesting and satisfying. They tended to become tiresome once the first surprise was over. But the *décor* was nearly always remarkable, and as examples I may mention Derain's *La Boutique Fantasque* (the marvellous tone of blue of its curtains is still vivid in my mind), a Braque ballet, Miro's *Jeux d'enfants*, the brilliant and bizarre mica setting of *Le Chat*, and Marie Laurencin's *Les Biches*. It will be noticed that most of these artists are French; in fact Diaghileff's aesthetic home was Paris, and his pictorial sense and almost infallible taste in all visual matters came to predominate in his later days when he had made Paris his headquarters.

The more dancing as such—especially classical dancing rather than miming—predominates in a ballet the more important does the music become and I confess I belong to those whose preference leans to the classical and musical side of ballet. Such ballets as *Giselle* or *Coppélia* or *Le Lac des Cygnes* would be completely spoiled by indifferent music. Delibes' music to *Coppélia* is absolutely brilliant, and unrivalled in its clean-cut inventiveness in melody and rhythm; outstanding also is his *Sylvia*, which ought to be revived. Another fine score is Stravinsky's *Le Baiser de la Fée* and—in a quite different style—his more dramatic pieces *Petrouchka*, *The Firebird* and *Le Sacre de Printemps*. Stravinsky is so far the greatest master of ballet music since Tchaikovsky, yet it is doubtful whether he has produced anything that will survive as long as Tchaikovsky's *Swan Lake*. This work of absolute genius has never received its due from the musicians and musical critics of our generation. It is too completely out of the temper of our times; but the fact that, notwithstanding, it has never failed during half a century to attract a large public is a sign of its rare power. Actually, it is a work of imagination of a very strange quality. I do not know of anything else in music quite like it.

Finally, I would go so far as to say that music is so essential a part of ballet that on it finally depends any ballet's lasting success. Everything else may be revised with a new *décor* and a new choreography from time to time but if the music is not of permanent value and interest then it will never be possible to make the ballet live.

MASSINE IN *TRICORNE*
Brush drawing by Theyre Lee-Elliott

THE MALE DANCER

A CERTAIN prejudice against ballet prevalent in Anglo-Saxon countries is based on the ignorant supposition in some quarters that the
role of a male dancer is a rather inglorious if not a feeble one for a
man. Like many such prejudices this has no solid foundation. Dancing
as a career makes greater physical demands on the rank and file than perhaps any other peace-time profession, and to achieve distinction in it requires not only an excellent physique but a discipline of mind and body
that far exceeds the average, in addition to artistic gifts. Nobody who has
seen that great dancer Leonid Massine—the greatest male dancer of our
time since Nijinsky—could ever harbour any such illusion again. The
physical stamina, to say nothing of the nervous energy and power of mind
over the body, displayed by Massine in most of his roles—such as *Le Beau*

Danube—far exceeds even that demanded in most athletic sporting events; while such a dance as that of the bar-tender in *Union Pacific* would be quite beyond the physical powers of most Olympic champions. It is true that dancers such as Nijinsky and Massine have greatly extended the scope of the old-time male dancer by enlarging the old-fashioned limits of ballet; but this only shows that the role of the male dancer very much depends on the dancer himself and what he can make of his profession. Perhaps there was a time in the nineteenth century, when owing to a concentration on mere virtuosity on points the male dancer sank into a minor role, due, only partly, to the undoubted male inferiority in toe-dancing. In fact he became known as "the ballerina's third leg" and a successful "third leg" was known professionally as a *danseur noble*. This limitation, however, disappeared with the fresh developments of the twentieth century which so greatly enlarged the customary limits of ballet, and thereby gave a new and increased importance to the male dancer. Such a role as Satan in the ballet *Job* is a good English example of this new development, a role requiring personality as well as physique.

RHYTHM

IN the equipment of a male dancer a fine sense of rhythm is at least as important as an exceptional physical equipment. It is not for nothing that a great dancer like Massine is a passionate lover of music, for without this special musical sense he could never have achieved his superb dancing performances. Melody and rhythm in music are so closely interwoven that I doubt whether a dancer insensitive to tone could ever go far, but certainly any deficiency in his rhythmic sense would be absolutely fatal, since dancing is essentially *visual rhythm*, i.e., rhythm seen in time and space; whereas, in the purely visual art of painting, an artist is only concerned with rhythm seen in space.

The average person's sense of rhythm is quite imperfectly developed both visually and aurally. This general insensitivity explains why most people prefer simple easy melodies in music, just as they prefer simple representation in painting. They just cannot grasp rhythmic complications either in space, as in painting where it vitalises 'design' or 'composition,' or in time as in music; but in the finest forms of ballet these two rhythmic spheres, 'time' and 'space,' are combined and, as I have already pointed out, the visual rhythms of the dancer's movement in space must coincide or agree harmoniously with the rhythms in sound, *i.e.*, the music. Moreover,

THE WEDDING BOUQUET

Sadler's Wells.   Ballet and music by Lord Berners.   London 1937

Study for the drop curtain by Lord Berners

By courtesy of John Carr Doughty, Esq.

THE PROSPECT BEFORE US

Sadler's Wells — Boyce (arranged by Lambert) — Ninette de Valois.   London 1940

in addition to the simple dancer's movements (which we may compare with a single tune or theme) there are spatial groupings of the *corps de ballet* and these must combine like counterpoints or a harmonic background to movements of the solo dancer—just as a musical theme is combined with other themes or harmonised into a musical composition. It should be clear, therefore, what a complex demand upon the ears and eyes of the spectator the art of ballet makes, and, as with all other arts, the more you know and the more you see and hear the more you are able to perceive and to enjoy.

BALLET TRAINING

THE reader who has got this far will begin to understand why it is that the training for a ballet-dancer must not only begin with childhood (about the age of ten), but also that it requires many years of arduous physical and intellectual study. An interesting account of a dancer's training is in Madame Karsavina's *Memoirs* from which, with her kind permission, I take the following. It relates how she became a pupil of the Imperial School of Ballet at St. Petersburg, now Leningrad:

"Early in August we came back to town. A petition was to be sent first to the school; only a matter of form. All the candidates had to go through a thorough examination, and comparatively few were accepted. The first year at school was a test of pupils' capacity, and at the end of the year the weak ones were weeded out. Those who did not show sufficient progress were dismissed, the best of the remaining numbers taken as boarders, tolerably good ones being given the chance of a second year as day pupils. On the morning of the examination, August 26th, 1894, I was beside myself with fear that I might yet be refused. My hair had been put in papers overnight. I could not drink my tea in the morning, neither could I eat anything. Even the new white frock and bronze shoes I had on for the occasion could not take my mind off the ordeal.

"On the way to school Mother took me to a hair-dresser. While he was arranging my hair, at that time cut in a fringe and in loose curls at the back, I grew more and more impatient. I kept asking Mother whether it was not yet time to go. When we arrived at the school, the sight of the beadle's livery with the Imperial eagles on it, made me feel very small. We left our coats and wrappings in the vast hall and went upstairs. On the way, Mother gave a final touch to my dress and hair, and said the white set off my sunburn very prettily. In the big room on the first floor there were already many small girls waiting. We waited for some time, and I took the opportunity of going round looking at the portraits of the Imperial family on the walls before a stern-looking lady in black sailed in with six other ladies in cashmere dresses of light blue. They were the directress and governesses. The lady in black went round, saying a few affable words to parents here and there. Mother had told me before that she was a distant relation, and I expected to be petted; but Varvara Ivanovna only looked at me with her cold grey eyes and exchanged greetings with Mother. The governesses arranged us in twos and marched us off to the next room, where benches were set on both sides and a row of tables and seats by the mirrored wall for the examiners. The doors were shut on the waiting parents. I saw Father sitting with other masters, but he did not give me any sign that he noticed me. A few names were read out at a time, and those called came into the middle of the room and stood there while the masters went round looking at them. We first stood still, then we were told to walk, then to run. That was to judge our looks and whether graceful or awkward children. Then we stood with heels together for our knees to be looked at. These preliminary tests took some time, as there were over thirty children. After the first test many were dismissed as unsuitable. Again we were arranged in twos and this time led through a long enfilade of classrooms to the infirmary to be examined by a doctor. We had to undress completely and were given some linen dressing gowns in which to wait for our turn. The examination was very thorough. Some children were dismissed on account of weak hearts; others had a slight deviation of the spine. Sight and hearing were tested too. When the doctor's examination was over, we were taken to the so-called "round room" and given some tea and sandwiches. During this interval for lunch Father looked in, and I ran to him, asking whether I was accepted. He put me off with his usual 'Who knows much . . .'

"After lunch the music mistress made us sing a scale to judge our ear for music. Examination in reading, writing and arithmetic followed. The final choice was yet to be made, as the number of pupils had to be limited. So we again were led to the big room where the dancing masters sat. Only ten were taken, and I was amongst them. By the time we came home it was six o'clock. All that had happened had to be lived through again in happy conversation. Mother wanted to find out from Father if the examiners were impressed by my looks. She maintained I was the best-dressed child of the whole lot. I also had to tell Lev and Douniasha how all went on and what was said to me and what the other children were like.

"The classes were to begin on September 1st, and in the few remaining days my school outfit was to be ready. It consisted of a brown cashmere for classes and a dancing frock of a special pattern in grey holland. Father took

Original sketch design
for a dress for
Mme Karsavina
Truth about the
Russian Dancers.
Coliseum. London
1920.

TAMARA KARSAVINA IN *THE TRUTH ABOUT THE RUSSIAN DANCERS*
A play with ballet by J. M. Barrie, 1920
Design by Paul Nash

me out to buy a school box. Particular joys to me were a satchel which I
chose in imitation of tiger skin and all the small requisites like the pen,
pen case and its fittings. I had a delightful feeling of property in handling
all these. Up till then I had never had a pencil I could call my own. We
lived a good way off from the school, and to get there in time I had to leave

the house with Father before eight. In those days we had no tramways, only street cars, pulled along the rails by a couple of horses.

"On arriving at the school the day pupils changed into dancing frocks on the entresol, under the auspices of a tiny grey-haired, mousy-looking, kindly old woman and went straight upstairs to curtsy to the governess and then in to the smaller practice room. The dancing classes were held in the morning. We then changed and had lunch in the round room. Tea was provided by the school, but we had to bring our own sandwiches. Sometimes, in the way of a treat, Father would buy me some hot jam pies from the arcade of the Gostinoy Dvor close by. Gourian, the beadle, handed me the little parcels 'from Papa. The pies were of rich pastry, delicious, though highly indigestible.

" 'Theatre Street' will always remain to me a masterpiece of architecture. I could not then analyse the beauty of my surroundings, but I felt it, and it grew on me as the time went on."

THE TECHNIQUE OF DANCING

TO those interested in ballet-dancing technique I recommend a little book by Kay Ambrose, entitled *The Ballet-Lover's Pocket Book*. The author of this book is an excellent draughtsman and he gives a large number of diagrammatic drawings which show the five positions of the feet, with the arms, which are the first elements of classical ballet-dancing, and then goes on to describe all the steps, and combinations of leg and arm movements, which are the technical foundation of choreography, and may be likened to the major and minor scales of music. To give a mere list of all these with their conventional French names such as *battements*, *ronds*, *entrechats*, *fouettés*, *arabesques*, *attitudes*, *poses*, *ballottés*, etc. would be useless without illustrations, and also out of place here as I am not writing a technical handbook on the ballet but a critical appreciation of the art. But this is the place for some general observations.

Just as in music, or in any other art, technique is the beginning and not the end, and a point is quickly reached (unless the student altogether lacks the primary natural gifts for his chosen study) when it becomes no longer possible to separate the technique from the art and make any further progress. There are always, of course, people who become so proficient in certain aspects of technique owing to natural gifts (and, I would add, even natural deficiencies also—although this is never understood by dilettantes)

that they become virtuosos; that is to say they can do quite easily, and apparently with less real effort, what others find difficult. But virtuosity as such should never be visible or audible in any artistic effect, for the artist is not yet fully qualified who lets his difficulties appear in his performance; so that, strictly speaking, the virtuoso is or should be only discernible to the expert. If the layman can perceive his virtuosity then this performer is certainly a bad artist whatever his technical prowess. But as the world becomes increasingly full of ignorant time-killers who lower the standard wherever they put in an appearance this bad artistry of visible virtuosity gets the plaudits of the unenlightened and unperceptive; which means that bad artists are commonly mistaken for good, and the superior ones stay unappreciated simply because they are literally, less showy.

It is when a dancer's body has been fully trained to carry out smoothly and gracefully the demands made upon it in all the traditional steps and movements of classical ballet, *i.e.* when it can execute decently the achievements of former masters of the dance, that the student begins his develop-

37

ment from a student into an artist, and it is just here that so many technical prodigies fail—exactly as in the sister arts of painting, music, and even literature. What it is that makes the truly outstanding and genuine artist is exceedingly difficult to define in a few words. Asked to put it into two words I would say *sensibility* and *power;* into one word *personality*. There is a superb saying, by that fine French poet, Charles Péguy, which puts the matter into a nutshell. Speaking of people who say the same things (just as dancers dance the same roles—Giselle, Coppélia, etc.—and musicians play the same music—Mozart, Beethoven, etc.) Peguy remarks "One man tears the words from his guts the other pulls them out of his overcoat pocket."

Nothing need be added to that. It is a basic verity, and one, unfortunately, that is least often remembered.

OUR NATIONAL BALLET

AS we have already seen our own ballet dates from the Russian Ballet of Diaghileff. As recently as 1920 that famous dancer Adeline Genée founded in London the Association of Operatic Dancing, now under Royal Charter as the Royal Academy of Dancing, and in 1922 the Cecchetti Society was started, the committee including Ninette de Valois and Marie Rambert who have both maintained schools of ballet-dancing in London, as did Astafieva, who was responsible for the first appearance of Patrick Kay (known as Anton Dolin) and Alice Marks (later Markova). It was in 1931 that the Sadler's Wells Ballet Company began functioning under Ninette de Valois. Ever since that time there has been a continuous output of new ballets by English choreographers, working with English dancers, musicians and artists. In the thirteen years from 1931 to 1944 several gifted British choreographers have won an assured position: Ninette de Valois, Frederick Ashton and Robert Helpmann, and, I would add, Andrée Howard. Here are some dates with a brief commentary on the principal original productions of these three choreographers :

I NINETTE DE VALOIS
The Rake's Progress
Décor by Rex Whistler, after Hogarth, music by Gavin Gordon; Sadler's Wells 1935-6
The Haunted Ballroom
Décor by Motley; music by Geoffrey Toye; Sadler's Wells 1935-6
Job
Décor by Gwendoline Raverat, after Blake; music by Vaughan Williams, orchestrated by Constant Lambert; 1931

FAÇADE: THE LADY AT THE WINDOW, DESIGN BY JOHN ARMSTRONG

The Gods go A-Begging
Décor by Hugh Stevenson; music by Handel, arranged by Sir Thomas Beecham; Sadler's Wells 1934
Checkmate
Décor by Edward McKnight Kauffer; music by Arthur Bliss; Sadler's Wells 1937
The Prospect Before Us
Décor by Roger Furse; music by William Boyce (1710-79) arranged by Constant Lambert; Sadler's Wells 1940
Promenade
Décor by Hugh Stevenson; music by Haydn, arranged by E. Evans; Sadler's Wells 1943

II FREDERICK ASHTON

Frederick Ashton devised the choreography of a number of ballets for Marie Rambert, the Ballet Club, and for the Camargo Society before going to Sadler's Wells, I note here only a few of his chief ballets:

Façade
Décor by John Armstrong (Mr. Armstrong's second version was in my opinion inferior to his original one) music by William Walton; 1931
Rio Grande
Décor by Edward Burra; music by Constant Lambert; 1931
Les Rendezvous
Décor by William Chappell; music by Auber, arranged Lambert 1936
Le Baiser de la Fée
Décor by S. Fedorovitch; music by Stravinsky; Sadler's Wells 1935
Apparitions
Décor by Cecil Beaton; music by Liszt, orchestrated by Gordon Jacob; Sadler's Wells 1936
Nocturne
Décor by S. Fedorovitch; music by Delius (Paris); Sadler's Wells 1936
Les Patineurs
Décor by W. Chappell; music by Meyerbeer, arranged by Lambert; Sadler's Wells 1937
Wedding Bouquet
Décor and music by Lord Berners; Sadler's Wells 1937
Horoscope
Décor by S. Fedorovitch; music by Lambert; Sadler's Wells 1938
Dante Sonata
Décor by S. Fedorovitch, after Flaxman; music by Liszt; Sadler's Wells 1940

HAMLET

Sadler's Wells — Tchaikovsky — Helpmann.   London 1942

Design for the set by Leslie Hurry

THE QUEST

Sadler's Wells — Walton — Ashton.   London 1943

Design for the backcloth. Scene III   by John Piper

The Wanderer
Décor by Graham Sutherland; music by Schubert; Sadler's Wells 1940
Wise and Foolish Virgins
Décor by Rex Whistler; music by J. S. Bach, arranged by Walton; Sadler's Wells 1940
The Quest
Décor by John Piper; music by William Walton; Sadler's Wells 1943

III ROBERT HELPMANN

Comus
Décor by Oliver Messel; music by Purcell arranged Lambert; Sadler's Wells 1943
Hamlet
Décor by Leslie Hurry; music by Tchaikovsky; Sadler's Wells 1943
The Birds
Décor by Chiang Yee; music by Respighi; Sadler's Wells 1944

IV ANDREE HOWARD

Lady into Fox
Décor by Nadia Benois; music by Honegger; Ballet Rambert 1939
Le Festin de l'Araignée
Décor by Michael Ayrton; music by Albert Roussel; Sadler's Wells, 1944

English Ballet is now a clearly established form of artistic entertainment and its wide increase in popularity has been helped by the touring of the provinces during the war by various companies, including the Sadler's Wells company, the Marie Rambert company, the Anglo-Polish Ballet and others. In spite of all the difficulties the war has brought about it has also accelerated the increase in public interest, even though that was already advancing rapidly by 1939. This increase in popularity was recognised by the fact that, already in the year 1939, a scheme of development had been proposed consisting of:

(a) An enlargement of the Sadler's Wells school and formation of a second company.
(b) Ivitation to a new British choreographer every year to produce at least one experimental ballet.
(c) Invitation for a two-year period of some eminent choreographer to introduce new ideas.

Such a plan is essential to the prosperous development of ballet in this country and it is to be hoped that it will quickly be put into operation as soon as the present war is over.

HAROLD TURNER IN *LES PATINEURS*
Gouache by Theyre Lee-Elliott

THE SADLER'S WELLS COMPANY

IT is necessary to give a few more details of the English company which had established itself on a permanent basis at Sadler's Wells and can thus claim to be the first National Ballet we have ever possessed in this country. Since the present war began it has lost its permanent home at the Sadler's Wells theatre, which was closed in September 1940. But it will, no doubt, return there when the war is over. After the company's escape from Holland, where it was on tour, as has already been described, it found in 1941 a fresh headquarters at the New Theatre in St. Martin's Lane where it has been appearing ever since, at intervals sharing this theatre with the dramatic company from the 'Old Vic,' and alternating between London and our provincial towns. The original ballet company which was formed in 1931 consisted at that time of about eleven members.

Margot Fonteyn in *Nocturne*
Gouache by Theyre Lee-Elliott

After Markova's departure in 1935 its leading members were Pearl Argyle, June Brae, Alan Carter, William Chappell, Margot Fonteyn, Robert Helpmann, Pamela May, Elizabeth Miller, Claude Newman, Harold Turner and Michael Somes. In 1943 the Company had increased to thirty-five members with the following staff:

> Director—Ninette de Valois
> Ballet Mistress—Joy Newton
> Academic Tuition—Peggy Van Praagh
> Musical Director—Constant Lambert
> Conductors—Constant Lambert and Julian Clifford
> Stage Director—Henry Arneil
> Stage Manager—Henry Robinson

Margot Fonteyn has developed into a brilliant exponent of the leading classical roles such as Giselle, Swanhilda in *Coppélia*, Aurora in *The Sleeping Princess* and Odette in *Le Lac des Cygnes*. Other members who have made great progress are Beryl Grey and Alexis Rassine, while Robert Helpmann and Andrée Howard as choreographers have made up for the temporary loss of Frederick Ashton. But quite apart from the fact that excellent soloists have emerged during the ten years existence of the company a definite character and *esprit de corps* has already developed and the foundation of a National Ballet may be said to have been well and truly laid, based on the large classical repertory. In addition, a remarkable repertory of new ballets by English choreographers, with scenery and costumes by English artists, and music by English composers, has been produced. Fresh young dancers are continually coming forward from the Sadler's Wells training school and from other ballet training schools, such as Marie Rambert's, so that the Sadler's Wells Ballet may now be said to be thoroughly national and self-supporting both as regards its dancers, and its choreographers, artists and composers.

NATIONAL CHARACTERISTICS

NATIONAL characteristics undoubtedly show themselves in all the arts, though it may be true that they tend to disappear at the highest levels. But whenever genuine national characteristics exist they arise spontaneously and unconsciously and are never achieved by deliberate seeking. When deliberately sought the invariable result is artificiality and dullness. The national character of Diaghileff's famous Russian Ballet was not

LE SPECTRE DE LA ROSE
The young girl's white ball dress
Design by Rex Whistler

due to a concentration on Russian themes, or Russian folk dances, or old Russian national costumes; quite the contrary, for Diaghileff often deliberately chose subjects that were not specifically Russian—such as *Les Sylphides*, *Le Spectre de la Rose* (in which Nijinsky achieved one of his greatest triumphs) *Carnaval*, *La Boutique Fantasque*, *Tricorne*, etc. In fact he went to France, Italy and Spain for many of his ideas, his artists and his musicians; but nevertheless the result always had a character of its own

45

COPPELIA
Design for the set, Act III by William Chappell

as it passed through a sort of artistic transformation by his company under his direction. His principal dancers had been through the famous Russian State Ballet-school, but even this school was the product of Italian and French teachers and only gradually evolved into a Russian school, a new combination of mixed influences, both the Italian and the French schools having in the course of time degenerated into static repetition. Mr. Arnold Haskell writing in 1943 says:

"When some years ago I visited the Scala, Milan, I was amazed at the classical ballets I saw; it was a technique so very different, yet so slick and competent that I felt I was watching something totally unfamiliar. The choreography was nothing but an exploitation of that *staccato* graceless acrobatic technique and the dancers' legs would have supported a concert-grand."

Physical as well as temperamental differences contribute to a national style. English dancers in general are of more slender, more graceful, more mobile physique than Italian and French dancers. You will not find among them—men or women—these grand-piano legs. Also they have a quite individual sensibility and subtlety. As a rule they under-emphasize, rather than exaggerate, and an English *corps de ballet* has a delightful fluidity that is entirely its own. Our choreographers also show, quite unconsciously,

46

LE FESTIN DE L'ARAIGNEE
Design for the costume of the Praying Mantis by Michael Ayrton

similar national characteristics. For instance, Frederick Ashton's fascinating ballet *Le Baiser de la Fée* has this sensitive, evanescent English fluidity, yet the music is by a Russian, Stravinsky, and so are the costumes (Fedorovitch). The same material handled by Italian, Polish or Russian choreographers would have been given by each a quite different atmosphere. The same is true of that charming ballet, also by Ashton, *Les Patineurs*.

The temper of the English people, is, on the whole, quieter, more delicately shaded and less vivid than that of the Americans or the Latins. Mr. Haskell thinks that in ballet-dancing we resemble the Russians more than any other people. A definite affinity between the English and the Russian temperament has often been suggested by writers who know both countries well. It finds support in a number of facts, of which I shall only mention one. In no other country have the great Russian authors found so large, sympathetic and even enthusiastic a reading public as in England. And if we take as examples two of the most outstanding Russian authors, Tolstoy and Tchekhov, we have to admit that Tolstoy in his preoccupation with moral problems strikes a particularly English note, while the tolerant, unfanatical Tchekhov seems more English than the English; and it is significant that he has never attained either the popularity or the reputation in Germany that his work has enjoyed in this country.

47

It is worth while concluding here with a quotation from a plan for the reform of the ballet submitted to the director of the Russian Imperial Theatres in St. Petersburg by Michel Fokine, the choreographer of *Les Sylphides, Schéhérazade, L'Oiseau de Feu, Petrouchka* and many other famous ballets.

"Dancing should be interpretation. It should not degenerate into mere gymnastics. The dance should explain the spirit of the actors in the spectacle. More than that it should express the whole epoch to which the subject of the ballet belongs.

"For such interpretative dancing the music must be equally inspired. In place of the old-time waltzes, polkas, *pizzicati*, and *galops*, it is necessary to create a form of music which expresses the emotion as that which inspires the movements of the dancer.

"The ballet must no longer be made up of 'numbers,' 'entries,' and so on. It must show artistic unity of conception. The action of the ballet must never be interrupted to allow the dancer to respond to the applause of the public.

"In place of the traditional dualism, the ballet must have complete unity of expression, a unity which is made up of a harmonious blending of the three elements—music, painting, and plastic art."

These sound principles enunciated by Fokine are of international validity and hold good for the art of the ballet in every nation.

SHORT BIBLIOGRAPHY

Arnold L. Haskell :
Balletomania, Gollancz. *Dancing Round the World*, Gollancz. *Prelude to Ballet*, Nelson. *Balletomane's Scrapbook*, A. & C. Black. *Balletomane's Album*, A. & C. Black.

Cyril W. Beaumont :
Complete Book of Ballets, Putnam. *A French-English Dictionary of Terms used in Classical Ballet*, Beaumont. *The Ballet called Giselle*, Beaumont.

Kay Ambrose :
The Ballet-Lover's Pocket Book, A. & C. Black.

Tamara Karsavina :
Theatre Street, Heinemann.